WILLIAM H. WILLIMON

LEADER'S GUIDE
BY M. KATHRYN ARMISTEAD

THIS WE BELIEVE

THE CORE OF WESLEYAN
FAITH AND PRACTICE

IDEAL FOR USE WITH
The WESLEY STUDY BIBLE

Abingdon Press
Nashville

THIS WE BELIEVE
LEADER'S GUIDE

10 11 12 13 14 15 16 17 18 19—10 9 8 7 6 5 4 3 2 1

MANUFACTURED IN THE UNITED STATES OF AMERICA

A WORD TO LEADERS

*T*his *We Believe: The Core of Wesleyan Faith and Practice* is an eight-week study for adult groups. Its purpose is to provide participants with information about fundamental Methodist beliefs in order to help them live more faithfully as disciples of Jesus Christ. This study is designed to give guidance for interpreting the Scripture within a Methodist/Wesleyan framework, which will help people live the abundant life that Jesus promises. Many of these basic beliefs are spelled out in the Core Terms found in *The Wesley Study Bible*.

As group leader, you facilitate each session using this leader's guide. You will need a copy of *This We Believe: The Core of Wesleyan Faith and Practice* and, for best results, a *Wesley Study Bible* for each participant, and a chart or board with appropriate writing instruments for group activities.

Throughout the book, Bishop Willimon refers to the Core Terms that appear as sidebars within the notes of *The Wesley Study Bible*. In the book, the Core Terms are noted with the page number on which they appear in the Bible. They are meant to help people understand the basics of our faith. For your convenience, they are also listed by biblical book and in alphabetical order in the back of the *WSB*. Just as John Wesley sought to speak as plainly as possible, these brief explanations will help people apply their faith to their daily lives.

You, as leader, might want to make a list of the Core Terms referred to in each chapter and read them ahead of time. They will be a valued resource for you as you study, plan, and lead the sessions. They will also help you keep the discussion focused.

Because no two groups are alike, this guide has been designed to give you flexibility in tailoring the sessions to your needs. You may use the following suggested format, *or adapt it as you wish to meet the schedule and needs of your particular group.*

Suggested Format	(40–50 minutes)
Sharing Prayer Concerns	(5–6 minutes)
Opening Prayer	(1–2 minutes)
Icebreaker	(10 minutes)
Scripture Reading	(3–5 minutes)
Group Discussion	(20–25 minutes)
Closing Prayer	(1–2 minutes)

Here are a few helpful hints for preparing and leading your group sessions:

❏ Read the corresponding chapter in *This We Believe: The Core of Wesleyan Faith and Practice* to the group session. Make note of the scripture references and core terms.

❏ Be the first person at the session. Arrive at least five minutes early, so you can welcome persons as they come in. Practice gracious hospitality. Begin and end on time.

❏ Introduce guests, help them feel welcome, and keep the business of the group short.

❏ Create a climate of participation, encouraging individuals to participate in ways that are comfortable for them. Some people are uncomfortable talking, so occasionally let them write their responses. If no one answers at first, don't be afraid of a little silence. Count to seven silently; then say something such as, "Would anyone like to go first?" If no one responds, venture an answer yourself. (Prepare your answer ahead of time.) Then ask for comments and other responses.

❏ Model openness as you share with the group. Group members will follow your example. If you share only at a surface level, everyone else will follow suit. If you want a richer discussion, you need to share at a deeper level.

❏ Be aware, however, that it is natural for the conversation to begin at a surface level and then move more deeply as the session goes on.

❏ Draw out participants without asking them to share what they are unwilling to share. Make eye contact with someone and say something such as, "How about someone else?"

❏ Encourage multiple responses before moving on. If you want more conversation around a response, ask something like, "Has that ever happened to anyone else?"

❏ Consider giving your answer first and then just going around the circle if you have trouble getting responses from the group.

❏ Avoid asking, "Why?" or "Why do you believe that?" Instead consider asking or giving an example to illustrate the point.

❏ Affirm others' responses with comments such as "Great," or "Thanks," or "I like that"—especially if this is the first time someone has spoken during the group session. Steer the conversation away from argument. If you feel things heating up, say something like, "You seem to feel strongly about this."

❏ Give everyone a chance to talk, but keep the conversation moving. Moderate to prevent a few individuals from doing all of the talking. Please note that some people will not talk unless you call on them.

❏ Monitor your own contributions. If you are doing most of the talking, back off.

❏ Remember that you do not have to have all the answers. Your job is to keep the discussion going and encourage participation.

❏ Before each group session, pray for God's presence, guidance, and power throughout the study. Pray for your group members by name and for what God may do in their lives.

It takes a dedicated leader to make any group session go well. Thank you for your commitment. Blessings on your ministry.

SESSION 1
INTRODUCTION

Sharing Prayer Concerns (5–6 minutes)
Opening Prayer (1–2 minutes)

Dear God, we really want to know you better, but we confess that sometimes it's just easier to turn away. Thank you for your faithfulness to us even when we are not as faithful as we need to be. But even when we turn from you, you are there pursuing us with your ever-seeking love. Be with those persons we've mentioned. Let them feel the presence of your Holy Spirit. But help us also do our part to help and comfort them. Now, we turn our hearts to you. Touch us, inspire us, lead us so that we might see just a glimpse of your glory. In Jesus' name, amen.

Introduction of Study (7–10 minutes)

To the leader: Take a few minutes to introduce this study at the first session.

John Wesley was the founder of the Methodist movement, begun in England in the eighteenth century. We, as United Methodists, are part of that heritage. For Wesley, the Bible is the joyfully consistent testimony of God's never-ending grace and ever-seeking love. Likewise, studying the Bible is more than merely knowing what Scripture says; it is also about living every day as a child of God. You might want to talk about why it is important to know what we as Christians believe.

Icebreaker (10 minutes)

Trust is fundamental to any relationship, including our relationship with God. When you were a child, who was the person you trusted the most? Share a time when you trusted someone with a secret. What happened? On a scale of one to ten (with one being low and ten being high), how trusting are you as a person? Take a few minutes and share with the group.

Scripture Reading (3–5 minutes)

Mark 10:17-31

Group Discussion (20–25 minutes)

1. People put their faith in all kinds of ordinary things, for example, car brakes, the availability of candy bars, and gravity. Share a time when you put your faith in someone or a time when someone put his or her faith in you. How easy is it for you to put faith in God's extraordinary love for you?

2. Who have been some of your faithful guides—a spouse, teacher, coworker, pastor, friend, child? How did they show you what it means to love God and neighbor? What did they do, and what did you learn from them?

3. Do you agree with Bishop Willimon's statement that "our God is so wonderfully complex, dynamic, mysterious, and counter to whom we expect God to be that you need help from your friends to think about the Trinity"? In your opinion, if there is value in group study, what is it? Share your most memorable group experience.

4. Bishop Willimon writes that Jesus never said, "Think about me!" He said, "Follow me!" What is the difference? Are you ready to follow Jesus more closely? What step could you take today that would lead you toward living a more grace-filled life?

5. Where do you need God's grace today? With whom do you need to share God's love today? Think of a relationship in your life that needs work. What can you do to let the love of God show through you to that person?

Closing Prayer (1–2 minutes)

Dear God, thank you for loving us and trusting us. Now empower us to follow you more faithfully. In Jesus' name, amen.

SESSION 2
WE BELIEVE IN ONE GOD—
FATHER, SON, AND HOLY SPIRIT

Sharing Prayer Concerns (5–6 minutes)

Opening Prayer (1–2 minutes)

Dear God, we thank you for showing us who you are in Jesus Christ. Everything we know about you comes from his life, death, and resurrection. And thank you for your generous gift of grace that helps us offer real and authentic prayers to you. We celebrate your power, justice, and righteousness; but today we want to especially thank you for your active, initiating, and ever-seeking love. We know that in the tough times, we can count on your promises to heal, guide, reconcile, and sustain us. Bless those we have mentioned, and let us now lift our hearts and turn our eyes upon you. In Jesus' name, amen.

Icebreaker (10 minutes)

Some people think of God as large, distant, and invisible. Others see God as a version of Santa Claus—perhaps even with a white beard. But in all cases, every one of us has some picture of God in our heads. Although we can't really see God, Jesus was fully human, a Jew born in Bethlehem. When you picture Jesus, who do you see? In your mind's eye, what does he look like? What color are his eyes, his hair? What is he wearing? What do his hands look like? Take a few minutes and share with the group.

Scripture Reading (3–5 minutes)

2 Corinthians 5:19; 1 John 4:7-21; Luke 15

Group Discussion (20–25 minutes)

1. Share a time that you lost something so valuable that you would not stop looking until you found it. If God never gives up on us, what does it say about God's active, initiating, seeking love? Is there someone in your life that you've been tempted to give up on?

2. According to Bishop Willimon, if God's love is more interesting, active, expansive, and determined than any human love, where would you like to see it in action? Where is God's love needed today in your life, your church, your neighborhood? If a person's relationships are shaped by love, what are the characteristics of those loving relationships? For example, how do you listen, how do you show you care, how do you set aside time for that person?

3. Understanding God as Father can be a problem for people who have had abusive or neglectful human fathers. Are there other ways to talk about God that might be more appropriate for those people? What was your father like, and how is God both like and unlike your dad?

7

4. John Wesley had a life-changing experience at Aldersgate. There, according to his own words, his heart was "strangely warmed." Share a time when you had a heartwarming experience. Share what happened to you or someone you know when she or he had a life-changing experience. How old were you? Where were you? What were the long-term consequences?

5. Most waiters and waitresses say the worst crowd to serve is the Sunday-after-church crowd. Why do you suppose this is? How could you show God's love to a stranger or family member today?

Closing Prayer (1–2 minutes)

Dear God, we praise you for giving us freedom to choose, and we pray that we find more ways to say yes to your ways. Be with us now as we depart to be your hands and feet in the world. In Jesus' name, amen.

SESSION 3
WE BELIEVE IN JESUS CHRIST AND HIS REIGN

Sharing Prayer Concerns (5–6 minutes)

Opening Prayer (1–2 minutes)

Dear God, we praise you for being the kind of God who finds us when we are lost, who redeems us when we sin, who restores us when we are broken, and who loves us when we are unlovely. Thank you for sending Jesus, who gave his life for us and our salvation. Because of Jesus, we can have eternal life beginning right now, here. We pray for those we have mentioned. Provide for their needs, and help us do our part to bring health and wholeness to our world. In Jesus' name, amen.

Icebreaker (10 minutes)

Share a time when someone made you feel that you were special. What did that person do? How did you respond? What have you done this week to make someone else feel special? Share a time when someone being with you made a big difference.

Scripture Reading (3–5 minutes)

Colossians 2:6-19; Romans 8:18-25; Matthew 6:9-15

Group Discussion (20–25 minutes)

1. Share a time when you *had* to be present for a special event. Why was it so important for you to make a personal appearance? Jesus is God's personal appearance. What real difference does it make to you that Jesus lived, died, and was resurrected? How is the world different as a result?

2. According to John Wesley, Jesus suffered and died for our sins, *and* through these great acts, *our capacity* to love God, neighbor, and

self is restored. What are the characteristics of God's love for us, for example, unconditional, merciful, patient, ever-seeking, eternal, freely given? Make your own list. How does your love align with God's love for you? Who do you need to love more like God loves? At home, work, school, play?

3. Before United Methodist pastors are ordained, they have to answer a series of questions before the Board of Ordained Ministry. One of these questions is, *What does it mean to say, "Jesus is Lord"?* If you had to stand before your friends and answer that question, what would you say? How would you begin? How is Jesus the Lord of your life today? Does that mean making any changes in your life?

4. Share a time when you tried a quick fix. What happened? What did you learn? The disciples wanted quick and easy answers too. How did Jesus respond to them?

5. Share your favorite story in the Bible about Jesus, or share your favorite story that Jesus told. What does it say about Jesus? What kinds of people were in his audience: the true believers, the skeptics, the ignorant, the powerful, the outcast, and so on? If you had been there, what group would you have been in? Do you think that Jesus had a sense of humor, a sense of wonder, and a sense of amusement? Do you think that Jesus was savvy about people? Why or why not? What kinds of qualities did Jesus value in his disciples?

Closing Prayer (1–2 minutes)

Dear God, let us depart from this place refreshed and renewed, with a right spirit within us. To you be the glory and honor. In Jesus' name, amen.

SESSION 4
WE BELIEVE IN THE WORK OF THE HOLY SPIRIT

Sharing Prayer Concerns (5–6 minutes)

Opening Prayer (1–2 minutes)

Dear God, we confess that most of the time we are in too much of a hurry. Help us slow down and focus on you for these next moments. Watch over us and our loved ones. Be with those we have mentioned who need a special word from you today. May the dove of your Spirit rest upon us as we discuss and learn more about you. In Jesus' name, amen.

Icebreaker (10 minutes)

Share a time when you were in so much of a hurry that you forgot or overlooked something. What are some ways that you relax?

Scripture Reading (3–5 minutes)

Mark 1:9-11; Acts 2; Luke 4:14-30

Group Discussion (20–25 minutes)

1. In John 3, Jesus refers to the Spirit of God as the wind. We have all been out in the wind, perhaps on a boat, in a car with the windows down, on a hill flying a kite as a kid, or in the eye of a storm. Share a time when you were in the wind. What was it like? How is the wind you experienced both like and unlike the Holy Spirit?

2. Share a time when you or someone you know had to be first, for example, first to speak, first to step forward, first to volunteer, first to say no, first to laugh. Sometimes it seems that some people always make the first move and others wait until the first move is made. Where do you see yourself? What might it say about God that God is willing to make the first move toward us?

3. Prevenient grace is a sign of God's ever-seeking love, and it is a very important part of our United Methodist thinking about God. Prevenient grace is God's freely given, unearned gift of God's love to us. Why might that be important to understanding who we are as a people of God? How might prevenient grace and Christian mission be related? Have you ever given a gift to someone for no reason, "just because"? How did he or she respond? Is it easier for you to give or to receive? Have you ever seen God's prevenient grace at work in someone's life?

4. For Wesleyans it is never enough simply to say, "God is love." We must also note that God is redeeming, justifying love, love in action, love on the move toward us. When God justifies us, God is bringing us back into alignment with God's plan and purposes. How might your life be different if you were completely aligned with God? Would this realignment help you think or do things differently?

5. Share a time when someone made you feel like a "somebody" or when someone made you feel loved and appreciated. Who have you made to feel special lately? Loneliness is one of the major social ills of our time. Who needs you to reach out to them?

6. John Wesley often talked about being on the road to perfection, by which he meant that God continues to actively work in us to make us more loving, faithful, and holy. Where are you on that road—at the beginning, middle, or end? What have been some of the obstacles or milestones of your life's journey?

Closing Prayer (1–2 minutes)

Dear God, help us see your loving care for us. Help us be your loving care for others. Help our voices reflect your loving Spirit. Help us refrain from gossip and hurtful jibes and comments. Help us build others up so that your kingdom may reign here on earth as it does in heaven. Now, free us for joyful obedience as we leave this place. In Jesus' name, amen.

SESSION 5
WE BELIEVE IN THE GUIDANCE OF SCRIPTURE

Sharing Prayer Concerns (5–6 minutes)

Opening Prayer (1–2 minutes)

Dear God, we thank you for the guidance of the Bible and what it means to Christians all around the world. Yet we confess that we haven't read it as we should and that we don't understand it as we might. Prepare our hearts and minds to be more receptive to your word. Let us not use the Bible as a way to divide us or as a weapon to enable conflict. Lord, we long to experience you and hear the good news. Please be with those we have lifted up in prayer, and help us turn to you in our hour of need. In Jesus' name, amen.

Icebreaker (10 minutes)

Share with the group the number of Bibles you personally own. How many Bibles are in your household? Which is your favorite Bible, and why?

Scripture Reading (3–5 minutes)

1 John 1:1–4; Nehemiah 8:1–3; 1 Corinthians 1:18–31

Group Discussion (20–25 minutes)

1. Share your favorite Bible verse or story. Why is it your favorite? What stories make you laugh or cry when you read the Bible?

2. Share a time when you felt humble. Hearing God's word in Scripture requires humble listening, informed discernment, and prayerful searching. In what ways and through what spiritual disciplines are you seeking to become more humble, informed, and prayerful? Would you like to learn more about spiritual disciplines, for example, prayer, fasting, tithing, acts of mercy and justice, study?

3. Pick a Bible verse as a group and commit to memorizing it.

4. Scripture is not just to be understood, pondered, and debated. According to Bishop Willimon, it is also meant to be enacted, embodied, and performed. As a person, are you more prone to pondering and debating or acting and embodying the Scripture? What Bible characters do you admire and strive to be like? What passages from the Bible trouble you? Inspire you? Motivate you?

5. Scripture is the account of an adventure, not a report on having arrived at a destination. On a scale of one to ten (one being low and ten

being high) how exciting has your faith journey been? Share a time in your life when your faith made a difference to you or those around you. Name a person in your life who encourages you or prompts you to be a better Christian.

6. According to 2 Timothy, the Scripture is meant to equip you for every good work. What good work are you currently doing? What good work is your church doing? How different would your community be if your church was not there? How can your friends tell that you are a Christian?

7. Make a list of your questions about the Bible. What book of the Bible would you like to know more about? What book of the Bible would you like to study with a group?

Closing Prayer (1–2 minutes)

Dear God, just as you inspired the writers of the Bible, inspire us to see you more clearly and follow you more nearly. Help us not be readers only, but also doers of the word. Let our lives reflect your peace, patience, kindness, goodness, gentleness, and self-control. Now free us for joyful obedience. In Jesus' name, amen.

SESSION 6
WE BELIEVE IN SALVATION FOR SINNERS

Sharing Prayer Concerns (5–6 minutes)

Opening Prayer (1–2 minutes)

Dear God, we thank you for being a relentless God, determined to save us even from ourselves. We confess that sometimes we need help. We need saving from our pride, envy, greed, laziness, fear, anger, apathy, violence, and dishonesty. God, sometimes it just seems that there is too much going wrong with too many people. Lord, we confess that sometimes we are so tangled up in our own stuff that we stop looking for you and your solutions. Be with us now as we lift up these people we have mentioned in prayer. And as we lift them up, let us also get a small glimpse of your throne to sustain us in our times of trouble. In Jesus' name, amen.

Icebreaker (10 minutes)

Share a time when you got lost—perhaps as a child or while driving to a destination. How did you feel? What did you do? How easy is it for you to ask for directions? How good are you at giving directions? Jesus can't save us unless we have a need. Knowing what you need is the first step to getting help.

Scripture Reading (3–5 minutes)

Luke 15

Group Discussion (20–25 minutes)

1. Share a time when you or someone you know needed saving, for example, from drowning, from the scene of an accident, from a poor choice, from a mistake. What happened? When Jesus saves us, what is he saving us from? What is he saving us for?

2. Jesus saves, but he was often accused (often by the religious people of his time) of wanting to save the wrong people. Who are the wrong people today? Are these people welcome in your church? Who are the people who are most welcome in your church, in your home? Do most of the cars in your church parking lot look similar? Would your church welcome all the people Jesus ministered to?

3. Share how you came to Christ.

4. The saying is, "Make a friend. Be a friend. Bring a friend to Christ." Are you making new friends? Suggestion: keep a prayer list of people you know who have no relationship with Christ. Make a commitment to pray for them daily for one year. You do not have to share the names on your list, but you can ask your group to keep you accountable for praying for them.

5. Share something with your group for which you need prayer. Pray for each member of your group, one at a time. Ask that each person would be strengthened and renewed in the image of God. You might ask the person being prayed for if she or he would like someone to lay hands on her or him while the group prays. Prayers can be done silently or out loud.

Closing Prayer (1–2 minutes)

Dear God, let us be peacemakers, let us be kingdom builders, and let us be united in one accord with the communion of saints. In Jesus' name, amen.

SESSION 7
WE BELIEVE IN CHRISTIAN WORK AND WITNESS

Sharing Prayer Concerns (5–6 minutes)

Opening Prayer (1–2 minutes)

Dear God, we confess that sometimes our busyness crowds you out of our lives. We get so intent on what we want that we quit listening to your voice and we quit reading your word. For these things, we ask forgiveness. Help us focus on you now, so that we can learn ways to put ourselves aside and receive the richness of your presence. Thank you for sticking by us, providing for us, and abiding with us. Please be with those persons we have lifted up. Sustain them, and guide us to be your ministers. In Jesus' name, amen.

Icebreaker (10 minutes)

Wesley talked a lot about the means of grace. By that he meant those things that feed our desire to do good in return for the good that God is doing among us. Share a time when someone did you a favor or a time that you did someone else a favor. Why did that person or you do it? What was your response? *Or* as you look around your church, share what you see that needs to be done or to happen.

Scripture Reading (3–5 minutes)

Leviticus 19:17-18; James 2:14-26

Group Discussion (20–25 minutes)

1. Share a time when you felt close to Christ.

2. As United Methodists, we believe in warm hearts with active hands. That statement is shorthand for our belief that God's love warms our hearts and that leads us to be God's active hands in the world. Where does your church, your community, need to see the love of God? Where are you and your church actively involved making the world a better place?

3. God empowers us with strength to go beyond our own power. What are you doing as an individual, group, or church that would be impossible except for the power of God? What would it be like for you and your church to try something that looks impossible without God?

4. Share a time when you either had a makeover or fixed something around the house, yard, or car. Why did you do it? God offers us restoration but also the gracious means to be more like God. If God gave you or your church a makeover, what might be different? Where might God begin? Changing attitudes, solving conflicts, sowing seeds of love?

5. Share your most memorable Communion experience. Share your baptism story.

6. Which of these practices is most helpful to you in your spiritual walk: reading Scripture; taking the sacrament; tithing; fasting; doing works of mercy or justice; visiting the sick, imprisoned, or older adults; going on mission trips; worshiping; doing something else?

Closing Prayer (1–2 minutes)

Dear God, send us from this place with a renewed sense of humility and assurance that what we do here matters. Help us remember that with you nothing is impossible. In Jesus' name, amen.

SESSION 8
WE BELIEVE IN THE GIFT OF THE CHURCH

Sharing Prayer Concerns (5–6 minutes)
Opening Prayer (1–2 minutes)

Dear God, you are the light of the world. For this we praise and thank you. You give us joy and peace. For this we praise and thank you. You give us your abiding presence. For this we praise and thank you. Now help us focus on you, so that we may deepen and enrich our gratitude and thankfulness. Be with those we have mentioned who need you in a special way this week, and bless us now as we lean in to listen for your voice. In Jesus' name, amen.

Icebreaker (10 minutes)

Share your favorite thing about your church and your small group.

Scripture Reading (3–5 minutes)

2 Corinthians 5:6-21; Galatians 5:22-23

Group Discussion (20–25 minutes)

1. Share why you are part of your church. What made you decide to make this church your church home?

2. On a scale of one to ten (one being low and ten being high), rate your church on these things: How loving is your church? How welcoming is your church? How generous is your church? How great is the worship at your church? How mission-oriented is your church? How spiritually fruitful is your church? Is your church growing in its love and service? How can your church help you become more welcoming, generous, worshipful, mission-oriented, and spiritually fruitful?

3. Is your life marked by the fruit of the Spirit as found in Galatians 5:22-23? Where are you most fruitful: love, joy, peace, patience, kindness, generosity, faithfulness, gentleness, self-control? Where would you like to be more fruitful?

4. The church is where we actively engage in the love of Christ in the world. Where is your church being a light to the world? Who has been helped because your church was there and cared?

5. If all power on heaven and earth was available to you, what would your church look like? What outreach would you do? Where would your church be located? What kinds of people would attend? Who would be your leaders? What kind of witness would you give?

6. United Methodist churches are connected to each other in purpose, mission, and ministry. How does your church take advantage of your connection to other United Methodist churches in your district, conference, jurisdiction? How does your church connect with other churches in your community?

7. Self-denial and simple living are messages that are often tough for people to hear, much less do. Share your thoughts and feelings about what it might mean for you to live more simply or with greater self-denial. Is this or should this be a part of Christian witness?

8. Take a few moments and reflect on your time with this study. What was most helpful? What was a big waste of time? Did it help or hinder you on your road to perfection? Are you better able to live a grace-filled life? Is your heart warmed, and are your hands active in mission?

Closing Prayer (1–2 minutes)

Dear God, we long to be your faithful witnesses. Give us the strength, courage, and perseverance to bring others to you. In Jesus' name, amen.